YOUR I

How to Create a
Vivid Vision
For Your Life
Live Your Life by Design
Instead of by Default

Michael E. Angier

Published by Success Networks International, Inc.
Spring Hill, Florida 34609-9509
www.SuccessNet.org

ISBN: 9781095184080

Limit of Liability/Disclaimer of Warranty

Professional Reviews

"We are often advised to set goals and then urged to take action to achieve those goals. In this book, Michael Angier takes us back a step by encouraging us to embrace a BOLD VISION for our best life before setting our goals. He artfully describes the importance of having a Best Life Statement. Michael encourages people of all ages—young and old—to deliberately create the vision for their life. This book is an easy read, yet inspirational. It causes you to think—about your life and what your best life looks like. As a consultant working with clients desiring strategic change in their businesses and life, I highly recommend How to Create a Vivid Vision for Your Life.*"*

—Judy Whalen, founder & CEO,
www.CenterForStrategicChange.com

"Vivid Vision offers guidance for anyone who wants to create a life plan and make it work. Initially, it looked like this is a work for young people who have only a limited sense of purpose and destiny. But it's really designed for anyone who wants to take command instead of just drifting along. Not only is it a quick, enjoyable read, Angier provides practical, actionable advice at every turn. Bravo. A fine addition to the wealth of materials Mr. Angier has already authored."

—Bob Jerus, SPHR, CEO of Success Dynamics
and author of the EIQ-2 Learning Systems

Foreword

By Dr. Philip E. Humbert

Most reviews describe what a book is *about*. They list the topics covered, tell you about the writing or endorse the content or author's perspective. I prefer reviews that describe a book's *impact*. What difference can a book make? What can it *produce*? These, to me, are the more important questions.

But to begin by following tradition, this book is about creating and living your very best life. Most people have lives of routine. Most days are taken up with work, family, paying bills, doing the ordinary tasks of life. Most people "get through the day." And generally, that works pretty well. Most people are neither miserable nor particularly excited, joyful or hugely successful. Michael's book uniquely seeks both to inspire greatness and to teach a simple but powerful way to rise far above the ordinary. Like a very few other short, powerful books (think James Allen's, *As A Man Thinketh* or Wallace Wattles', *The Science of Getting Rich), How to Create a Vivid Vision for Your Life* is destined to be a classic.

But more importantly, what can the book *do* for you? Let me tell you some of what it has already done for me. About five years ago, I largely retired from business and professional life. Then, a year after that, my beloved wife of 35 years was diagnosed with an incurable (and largely untreatable) illness. The past two years were entirely focused on caring for her as she deteriorated and then passed a few months ago. My sense of daily tasks, the sense of urgency, hard work, tangible goals and even my sense of self, related to my work, all evaporated. With her illness, my primary obsession became caring for her. Then, with her death, even that ended. Since then, I've committed to doing the work of grief, adjusting and coping with my new reality.

What I did *not* have was a vivid vision for any type of dynamic, exciting or challenging future. I was doing "OK." Friends told me I was even doing "remarkably well." But I knew, inside, that I was just treading water. I did my daily tasks, got my taxes done, took care of the house, but I was *existing*, not living anywhere near my potential. Then Michael sent me a draft of his newest book.

In the past 72 hours, I've got a whole new vision for my future! Sure, it's a preliminary, rough draft. It's "version 1a", if you will. But now I vividly see myself with a passion to share my experience with the many thousands of people who must cope with the illness and loss of a spouse. I see myself speaking to groups, perhaps writing my own book, coaching or consulting with thousands of people coping with the enormity of illness and loss. I will raise money, hopefully millions of dollars, for the treatment and (eventually) a cure for Parkinson's. In just days after reading this amazing book, I'm getting up earlier, smiling more, making phone calls, taking the actions that will create the new life I envision for myself. It's a "new me"!

Read and practice what this book recommends. It will, guaranteed, change your life. For me, it's given me a new, adventuresome, passionate and purposeful life. Let it do the same for you.

Table of Contents

Introduction

"Life is a great big canvas,
and you should throw all the
paint on it you can."
—Danny Kaye

Early in his young presidency, John F. Kennedy delivered a speech to a joint session of Congress. In it, JFK stated that the United States should set as a goal the "landing of a man on the moon and returning him safely to the earth" by the end of the decade.

Kennedy had not consulted with the scientists and engineers at NASA. And it's well that he didn't. They would have all told him it was impossible. The President must have known that you don't bring the problem-solving phase into the decision-making process.

It was a truly bold vision. At the time, we were very much behind in the space race with the Soviet Union. He didn't know how, and NASA didn't know how we would get it done.

And yet, in July of 1969, with less onboard computing power than we have in our smart phones today, Neil Armstrong and Edwin (Buzz) Aldrin landed and walked on the face of the moon. And they returned safely to earth, just as Kennedy (who had been assassinated six years before) had declared.

Michael E. Angier

What is Your Bold Vision?

This book is about a bold vision—a vivid vision—of your life the way you want it to be.

It's not about how to achieve it; it's about how to create the vision. And just like NASA, the how will come.

This is a time for clarity, about painting the picture of your ideal life.

You are the architect of your life. Your job is to design it first and build it later. So stay focused on the design. I encourage you to think big. Let your imagination soar.

The Blueprints

No one in their right mind would attempt to contract with a builder for a house without a plan—a detailed design, a clear picture and precise drawings of what is intended to be built.

And yet, people around the world set about their lives without planning sufficiently for how they want their life to be. They might have some vague notion, maybe a few goals or even a Bucket List. But only a tiny percentage of people (in my experience) have taken the time to envision their best life—living at their full and unique potential.

They live in reaction to the events in their life instead of being at source.

My Belief

There are things in this world which you and you alone are meant to accomplish. No one who has come before you, and no one who will come after, could be better qualified or as uniquely gifted to accomplish your unique purpose.

Think about it. With all the billions of people who have ever lived, and the billions that will eventually live on this beautiful planet, not one was—or will be—exactly like you.

You get to create your life—one day at a time, one month at a time, one year, one decade. This process of creating your vivid vision means beginning with the end in mind—as great as you can imagine it.

As I was writing this introduction, I saw a quote from Larry Winget—also known as the "Bulldog of Personal Development." He's a very direct, tell-it-like-it-is kind of guy and I respect him.

The quote was, "Nobody ever wrote down a plan to be broke, fat, lazy or stupid. Those things are what happen when you don't have a plan."

Of course, for purposes of this book, I would have used vision instead of plan, but you get the point, right?

"Nobody ever wrote down a plan to be broke, fat, lazy or stupid. Those things are what happen when you don't have a plan."
—Larry Winget

If you don't have a vivid vision (and a plan) for your life, you're going to fall into other people's plans. And you're not going to be too happy about that because they don't have much planned for you at all.

Michael E. Angier

Very Important Job

Creating a Vivid Vision for your Best Life is one of the most critical responsibilities you have. It will govern what you do, how you do things, when you do them and with whom you do them. It will determine how satisfied you are with the life you live. I cannot emphasize enough the critical nature of this process. You will not get a second chance at this life.

But What If I Don't Achieve My Vision?

Just in case you're thinking, "Wait, what if I do all this dreaming, imagining and envisioning and I just don't take any action—or I go for it and fail?"

Realizing your Best Life Vision is not guaranteed. You will fail to achieve some things. But failure is never final. Failure is an opportunity to learn. It's feedback—and feedback is the breakfast of champions.

If you *don't* set your sights high, if you *don't* go for it, I can guarantee that you will get less than you deserve. You will eventually choke on the dust of your own regrets. I don't think that's you. I'm betting you are much higher up on the Go-For-It scale than that.

With a Vivid Vision, you will be propelled into taking correct action, making good decisions and winning. You have created your vision of your life, and you will live into that inspiring vision from this point forward.

Are you ready? Let's get going.

Chapter 1
Your Best Life

---

*"We all have two choices: We
can make a living or we
can design a life."*
—Jim Rohn

Before we get into the nitty gritty of Your Vivid Vision, let's take a look at our objectives.

If you're reading this, I assume you want a better life. You want to improve on where you are. Maybe a little. Maybe a lot.

Regardless of where you find yourself at this point in time—and regardless of your age—you can certainly improve. After all, the biggest room in the world is the room for improvement.

You may be wanting to take your on-purpose, comfortable life and simply make it better. Or maybe your life is a train wreck.

Either way, you have to start with the end in mind.

It's important to acknowledge where you are, but there will be plenty of time for that. What's more important is getting clear on where you're going.

Your best life doesn't just happen. It doesn't automatically unfold, and it's certainly not given to you. You have to design and create your best life yourself. Because if you don't, other people and outside circumstances will do it for you. And remember what other people and outside circumstances have planned for you. Hardly anything at all.

What's Your Life Vision?

No doubt you have some idea about what your Best Life looks like. I assume you have some goals—some things you want to accomplish or experience before you make your departure from planet Earth.

Have you ever envisioned in great detail how you would like to have your life unfold? Do you see it? Can you taste it? Do you believe it?

The clearer you can become on all the things you want in your life—and the reasons why—the easier it will be to do what you need to do to achieve them.

We all want to be happy, and I personally believe we are happiest when we are in pursuit of our highest and best.

For now, let me share with you, in general terms, what I mean by your Best Life. It should give you some seminal ideas for your Best Life Vision.

"Your Best Life is a life with no regrets."

It's a tall order, but I think your Best Life is a life without regrets.

Your Best Life is a life by design, not default.

I think you should build a life you don't need a vacation from. Not that you won't *take* vacations, but you won't *need* them. Because your vocation will be your avocation. And it's not a struggle; it's a wiggle.

"Your Best Life requires your best self."

Your Best Life requires your best self. If you want your life to get better, *you* have to get better. I'm guessing that's why you're reading this book.

For me it means rising to a calling instead of an alarm clock. I get up when I *want* to get up, and very rarely do I use an alarm clock. It is possible.

I believe your Best Life is a life of clarity, purpose, passion and prosperity. A life designed around your values, principles and intentions.

Simply put—a life on your terms. You get to design, define, create and live Your Best Life.

Top Seven Results of Living Your Best Life
The following seven benefits are what I consider to be the biggest payoffs for having a life well lived.

1. Significance & Meaning

2. Time, Location & Financial Freedom

3. Happiness, Fun & Adventure

4. Purpose & Integrity

Michael E. Angier

5. Confidence & Self-esteem

6. Rich Relationships

7. Health, Fitness & Vitality

Sounds worthwhile, yes?

Your full and unique potential is unknown. But certainly worth going for, don't you think? Who can count the number of apples in a single apple seed?

"Death is not the greatest loss in life. The greatest loss is what dies inside us while we live."
—Norman Cousins

The Path to Your Best Life

The following illustration shows what I believe to be the best path to your best life—however you might define it. The bottom four tiers are foundational. The top three are much more dynamic. But they should stand in support of your core values, purpose, mission and vision.

Tasks
Projects
Goals
Vision
Mission
Purpose
Core Values

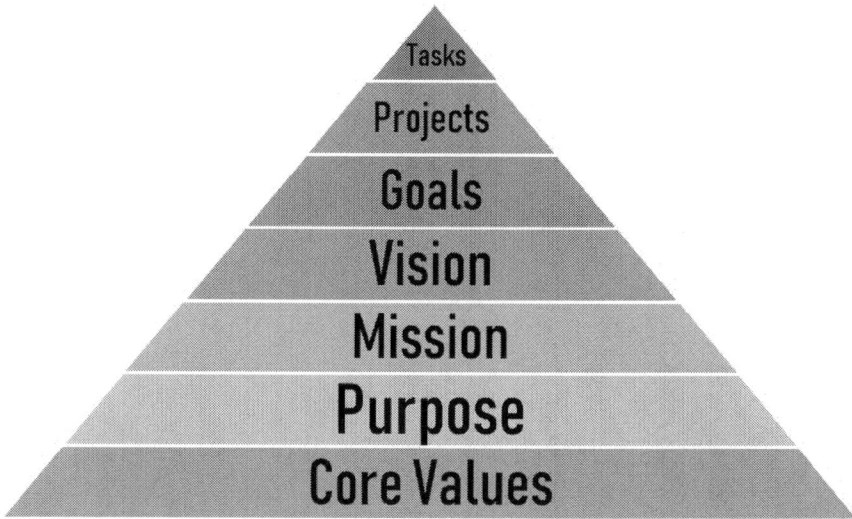

The Path to Your Best Life

My belief is that you can do anything in this life. But you can't do *everything*. And that's why it's so important to choose your vision, your goals and your projects wisely. And to base them on the foundational steps of core values, purpose, mission and vision.

Otherwise, you're making choices and spending your precious time and energy on your own or others' whims.

> *"Life should not be a journey to the grave with the intention of arriving safely in a pretty and well-preserved body, but rather to skid in broadside in a cloud of smoke, thoroughly used up, totally worn out, and loudly proclaiming 'Wow, what a ride!' "*
> —Hunter S. Thompson

These foundational steps are not within the scope of this book, but I strongly encourage you to think carefully about them. Getting clear on your core values, your purpose and your mission, will help you to avoid regrets and feel like you invested your life in the best way possible.

The bottom line is that unless you invest the time, energy and money in creating a life you truly want, you're going to be spending a lot of time and effort supporting a life you *don't* want.

Action Steps

Consider this home-study and video course on discovering and clarifying your core values. To find out more, go to www.YourCoreValues.com

Thousands of people have taken this course and benefited greatly from the process.

Chapter 2
Not Having a Vivid Vision Sucks

"The only thing worse than being blind is having sight but no vision."
—Helen Keller

OK, so you're reading a book about creating your Vivid Vision. And you've made it this far. Good for you.

You're probably thinking that you're pretty well sold on the value of this process and how you will live the life of your dreams.

But I ask you to take one more step with me.

What's a life *without* a Vivid Vision? Why does that suck?

Think about it. Most people do not have a Best Life Vision Statement. They spend more time planning their family vacations than they do planning their Best Life.

Look around. Most people's life is far less than great. Even the ones who seem to have it together, have good jobs, make descent money, etc., have far less success and happiness than they are capable of having.

Several studies in recent years here in the United States report that only about half of the people surveyed consider themselves happy—only *half*. And I would submit that less than half of *those* "happy" people would say they are living up to their full and unique potential.

Let's face it, most people simply drift through life. Taking what comes, complaining about it and surrendering to "The Rat Race". Maybe a goal here or a goal there, but mostly drifting.

They lack the planning, the belief, the confidence and the commitment to being a "10" on the Go-For-It Scale. As Henry David Thoreau wrote: "The mass of men lead lives of quiet desperation. What is called resignation is confirmed desperation."

At the very least, most people live by default instead of by design.

Life without a plan, life without purpose, life without a Vivid Vision is a waste.

On a more positive note, see what Henry David Thoreau had to say about a more directed life. The often-quoted first sentence is probably not new to you. But pay close attention to the rest of the quote and the promise it offers: "If one advances confidently in the direction of his dreams, and endeavors to live the life which he has imagined, he will meet with a success unexpected in common hours. He will put some things behind, will pass an invisible boundary; new, universal, and more liberal laws will begin to establish themselves around and within him; or old laws will be expanded and interpreted in his favor in a more liberal sense, and he will live with a license of a higher order of beings."

A "license of a higher order of beings". Take a moment and ponder that. It's pretty weighty stuff.

It sure beats the sucky, unplanned, uninspiring, unimpressive, unhappy, less-than-your-best, live-by-default life, yes?

Action Step

Commit to finishing this book and working through a plan for creating your Vivid Vision. You are worth it. Your best life is worth it.

You can always go back to not having a Vivid Vision, but please promise yourself you will finish this book and give it a shot.

Michael E. Angier

Chapter 3
You Gotta Believe

---

*"My interest is in the future because
I am going to spend the rest of my
life there."*
—Charles Kettering

O ne of the biggest hurdles most people have to overcome is to truly believe they can achieve what they really want to accomplish.

If someone else has achieved what you want to accomplish, you know it can be done. And if it's never been done, you can be the first.

Do whatever you need to do to get your belief to a point where you know you can live the life you imagine for yourself.

---

*"To accomplish great things, we
must not only act, but also dream;
not only plan, but also believe."*
—Anatole France

Be Like the Mets
In 1969, the New York Mets won the World Series.

Until then, this hapless team—only seven years old—had been the laughing stock of the league. One day, Tug McGraw, their pitcher, said to his team, "You gotta believe."

The media picked up on this. So did the fans. And that whole summer, the slogan became the mantra for what would eventually become a world championship.

So, like the Met's, You Gotta Believe.

Impossible You Say?

A long time ago, when my children were children, we encouraged them to utilize the dictionary often. We had a large one in the living room, and we all made good use of it.

This was, of course, way before spell check and online dictionaries.

One night at the dinner table, I told a story (I can't remember what it was) that sounded fantastical to these three young minds. One of them dismissed my story outright and said, "That's impossible."

To which I replied: "Impossible you say. That's an interesting word. I think you should look it up."

"We know what it means," they all said.

But I persisted. "Go ahead, look it up. Right now. I think you'll be surprised."

The oldest pushed back from the table and went to get the heavy dictionary. He brought it back to the table and when he found the word, he smiled and said, "It's not there. Instead, you made the word 'possible'."

He was right. I had redacted the IM in the word impossible so that only "possible" remained.

We then had a lively discussion as to whether or not anything is truly impossible. Because I'm not sure much of anything is.

I'm confident it made an impression on them.

These three children are all adults now, with children of their own. They all have college degrees, are thriving in their careers and doing work they love.

I can't take credit for their success. They earned that all on their own. But I do like to think that their "possibility thinking" played some part in them believing they could do anything they set their mind to.

Not long after that dinner conversation occurred, their mother and I, along with 120 others, walked barefoot on 1,200-degree coals with Tony Robbins. "The Fire Walk" expanded even more my thinking about what's possible and what isn't.

What seems impossible to *you*? Are you *sure* it's impossible?

If the word occurs in *your* dictionary, consider pronouncing it as "I'm Possible".

Action Step

Challenge yourself to think about your beliefs as to what's possible and what isn't. Give yourself permission to think *anything* is possible. What would you attempt to do if you knew you couldn't fail?

Michael E. Angier

Chapter 4
It's Never Too Late

"The best time to plant a tree was twenty years ago. The second best time is now."

—Chinese Proverb

Many people will think they are too old to create a Vivid Vision for their life. However, that's just not true.

Having a Vivid Vision earlier in your life would have been better, but you can't change the past. Even God can't do that.

You may not have control over what's happened, but you do have a good degree of control over what you do now and what you plan for the future.

You have exactly 100% of the rest of your life left. And you can make the rest of your life the best of your life.

These are not just platitudes; they are facts. But it's how you look at them—what you believe about them—that will determine the quality of your vision and the quality of the rest of your life.

Whether you are 21 or 81, the time you have left is unknown. All the more reason to make the best of it. Why not map out the remainder of your life? Make it what you truly want it to be.

I've always liked what Les Brown had to say about this: "You are never too old to set another goal or to dream a new dream."

And George Eliot who said, "It is never too late to be what you might have been."

Some Good Examples

Here are just a few people who were late bloomers—proving it's never too late.

Gramma Moses: A long-time embroiderer, she started painting at 75. Anna Mary Robertson Moses went on to sell over 3,600 paintings, most for only a few dollars apiece, but one sold for $1.2 million. She continued to paint until she was 101.

Colonel Sanders: If it hadn't been for Interstate 75 taking the traffic away from his popular restaurant, Harlan David Sanders would have been just a local legend. Instead, "The Colonel" started a franchise business and made millions for himself and for his franchisees.

Abraham Lincoln: The 16th president of the United States failed many times in very public ways. But he's certainly not remembered for that, is he? No, "Honest Abe" is considered to be one of our greatest presidents—and during a trying and tragic time in our history.

There are many others. And you would be wise to remember this when you think you might be starting late in the game.

Now, more than ever, we can rebound faster and bigger than we used to. Technology, communication, and quick and easy access to knowledge, funding and resources have made that so.

It's never too late to learn, too late to earn, or too late to create and live your own Vivid Vision and your Best Life.

How this Book Series Came to Be

A few years ago, I went into semi-retirement. I had achieved a fair amount of success, had simplified my life, and I took a sabbatical. I still wrote articles for our subscribers to SuccessNet.org, but mostly I took it pretty easy. I played tennis 4-5 times a week (still do) and I took what I thought was a well-deserved rest. It wasn't so much a conscious thing—I just slowed down.

But in reviewing my Life's Vision, my goals and my core values, I was reminded of a goal I had committed to achieving. It was to positively impact a million people before I die. Through sharing ideas, through inspiration and through encouragement, I wanted to help people live their best life.

It occurred to me that I wasn't sure I had reached a million people. And even if I had, why not reach a million more? I've not wanted to travel on the speaking circuit. I love our home and love being home. And I never liked schedules.

So writing books—especially short, topic-targeted books like this one—seemed a good choice.

And here we are. You are reading and hopefully writing, honing and living your Vivid Vision, and I am doing the same—partly through my writing. And because of my own Vivid Vision.

Michael E. Angier

Action Step

Do some thinking and maybe some journaling about dreams and goals you may have had but may have forgotten about. What have you filed away that you might want to rejuvenate into part of your vision?

What did you once discard as impossible that maybe now you think *could* be possible?

Chapter 5
Yes, You Do Deserve It

---

*"No matter how qualified or
deserving we are, we will never
reach a better life until we can
imagine it for ourselves and allow
ourselves to have it."*

—Richard Bach

What keeps many people from living their best life, and stops them from creating a Vivid Vision, is the sense they don't deserve having it.

And often coupled with that thinking is the erroneous belief that if they have a prosperous, abundant life, it will come at the expense of others. In other words, there is only so much wealth, money and happiness in the world to be carved up.

But believe me when I say you *do* deserve to dream big and live big. You deserve to have whatever you want in life.

And rest assured that you having more does not mean others will have less. That's not how economics works—at least in the long run.

One of the limiting beliefs held by many—either consciously or unconsciously—is that there is a finite supply of money. In other words, if one person has more, then that means someone else has less. That's simply not true, and I think the following story illustrates the point well.

Back in the eighties, Steven Clark Rockefeller built a house in Cornwall, Vermont—not far from where I grew up. It was reported to have cost a million dollars. Back then, a million-dollar home in Vermont was quite rare. It was a beauty, and I'm sure it's worth much more today.

My friend John Cady was one of the best commercial painters in northern Vermont, and he was fortunate enough to be awarded the painting contract for the Rockefeller home. I always thought it was interesting that he was paid with checks written on account number one of the Chase Manhattan Bank.

Stay with me here, as we see how wealth was not only moved to Vermont but also how it created even *more* wealth.

Before the house was built, Rockefeller had a million dollars in his family's bank in New York. After the house was built, he still had his million dollars; it's just that now it's in the form of a house. He exchanged his interest-earning million dollars for a million-dollar appreciating asset—his home.

Now here's where it gets interesting. This was not a tit-for-tat exchange. The million dollars was transformed—cash into real estate—but there was *also* now a million dollars in cash in the hands of contractors and building suppliers. That million was circulating through the Vermont economy and beyond.

A million dollars became two million dollars in the course of only a few months. Wealth was not only transferred—it was *created*.

No matter how successful you become, no matter how much wealth you may accumulate, never think you are taking it (unless you steal it) from others. In fact, your abundance enables you to do great things with it—including helping others. Sometimes directly, sometimes indirectly—like the Rockefeller story above.

Yes, you do deserve to create, live and enjoy your Vivid Vision for your Life.

Action Step

Search your thinking and beliefs about worthiness. Do you feel at all undeserving? If so, that's something to work on—something to overcome. Set about increasing your self-worth and self-esteem. It will make everything easier. Trust me that any feelings of unworthiness are erroneous.

Michael E. Angier

Chapter 6
My Vivid Vision

---

*"Where there is no vision,
the people perish."*
—Proverbs 29:18

I am sharing with you my personal Life Vision which I began writing over 30 years ago—in 1986. I've updated it over the years, but it's mostly as I originally wrote it.

And sometime during the last decade, it all came true—at least 95 percent of it. When I read through this document, it's abundantly clear that I am living the life I had envisioned.

That doesn't mean it's done. It doesn't mean I don't have more goals to achieve, more growth to experience and more to learn. But the essence and the experience of my life vision, as I had written it down, has been fulfilled.

I've edited out just a few personal details, but it is, for the most part, just as I had written and updated it over the years.

I share it with you to help stimulate your thinking and inspire your vision. Notice the present tense and descriptive languaging intended to invoke emotion.

My only suggestion is for you to dream bigger.

Financial & Career

We are completely debt free. Our financial commitments are always met on time. Our credit is excellent. We are rich, wealthy, and prosperous. There is always more than enough money to pay for all of our needs. I, therefore, live not in survival or maintenance, but in growth, fun, adventure, enlightenment, service, joy and my highest good. My financial security is in my ability to create for myself and my family all the money we need at the time we need it. I am in the flow of abundance—a co-creator with God. My success is absolutely assured. Our retirement is secure and abundant.

Our business is phenomenally successful and highly regarded throughout the world. It is a special source of pride and accomplishment. It provides us with a substantial income while furnishing us with the opportunity to be of service—creative, inspiring and influential. Our publications are always growing and prospering—adding value to everyone. They continually have a positive impact on the tens of thousands of people and businesses they serve.

Our business dealings are always performed with ease, excellence, elegance and integrity. We have fun, make lots of money and create exceptional opportunities for personal growth and development. Our cash flow is always more than sufficient to meet our needs. All our endeavors are meaningful and worthwhile—each of them moving us further and further to our highest good.

Our businesses provide us with the income, the security and the freedom to do what we love to do.

Family and Home

My relationship with my wife is the finest that I could have ever imagined. She is my best friend, lover, confidant and partner. We learn from each other all the time. We love, cherish and nurture one another in a way that's unequaled in any lifetime. Our trust, understanding, acceptance and faith in each other continues to grow. Our love and passion knows no bounds.

I am exceptionally proud of all of our children. There is great love, trust and respect between us. I listen to them and learn from them. They look to me for advice and guidance, and I give it with care and understanding. They all get along with each other and we thoroughly enjoy our time together.

My personal relationships are always ones of integrity, warmth, openness, inspiration, excitement, fun and education. No one is my enemy. Everyone is my teacher, causing me to see and understand myself more clearly. I have many friends from far and wide who support me and whom I unselfishly support with love, honesty, and affection. I make friends easily and effortlessly. Because I am present and at peace, I attract people to me.

We live in our beautiful, comfortable home with gorgeous views and other natural surroundings. Our home is a place of order, peace, cleanliness and safety. We feel comfortable and secure. I have a private study and office beautifully decorated in soft colors with lots of wood and plants. My study is quiet, well-lighted and inviting. There are floor-to-ceiling bookshelves, a desk and an inspiring reading area. It's a beautiful place to study, relax, write and create.

Our home has a warm, friendly atmosphere where people feel welcome and want to come often. There is a pool and a private yard with lots of plants and flowers. Tennis courts are nearby. Our large master bedroom suite provides us with peace, solitude and beauty.

Skills

I am an articulate and powerful speaker. My writing touches people, allowing them to see their higher selves and move them to action. My command of the English language is one of mastery. I always speak with good purpose using uplifting, encouraging words. What I write and speak is precise, inspiring and worthwhile. I am considered to be a sage and yet my humility stands above it. I deliver much of my wisdom on the wings of humor.

I practice first things first all the time. My life is organized, prioritized and on track. No one and nothing can take my good from me.

I am a very good tennis player (4.5 to 5.0).

Physical & Health

I fairly sizzle with zeal and enthusiasm. Perfect health flows through me and my family all the time. I have an abundance of strength, energy and vitality. I am attractive, powerful and healthy. I take good care of myself and support myself with forgiveness and reward. It is easy for me to maintain my perfect weight below 220 pounds while eating nutritiously and exercising regularly. I ingest into my body only those things that support this commitment. I look forward to living a long, prosperous and healthy earth life of at least 110 years.

Source

My interests are many and diverse and nourish all aspects of my life. I always have a sense of accomplishment because I'm always on purpose toward my highest good; growing and learning, always excited about what I'm involved in. I enjoy spending time with my many friends.

I make choices in my life that are for the good of all. I am involved in win/win situations all the time. I make these choices based on what is right and good rather than what is most expedient, profitable or easy. My choices are based on abundance—never on scarcity or fear. There are always plenty of choices and all my choices are good. There are no mistakes in the Universe. I live my life from choice—never obligation.

I have plenty of time to do the things I choose to do and are important to me. My life is organized and planned with everything in its place while still allowing for spontaneous happenings. Nothing *has* to be done. I am guided by God's wisdom all the time and make good decisions in all areas of my life. I am conscious of, trust, and listen to my inner voice. I exercise discipline with ease. I am efficient and effective, doing more and more with less and less. I live in the here and now: aware, alive, awake and full of life.

I consistently break through boundaries and barriers. With each accomplishment, I am able to see even more of myself and my potential. My joy knows no limits. I am constantly aware that I am a spiritual being choosing a human experience. I can do all things through the God within who strengthens me. I am uncovering more and more of my God self.

Worry is something I can only vaguely remember. I just don't do it. There is no fear in my life—only faith and love.

All of this is easy to accept as truth as long as I remember who I am and operate from the peace which comes from knowing this.

End of My Vision Statement

Believe me when I tell you that what you've just read is *nothing* like my life was when I wrote it. Since my original writing, I've been divorced, gone broke, filed bankruptcy, had some health scares and more.

At times when I would read this Vision Statement, it seemed that I was reading the complete opposite of my life. But I persevered—largely because of this Vision—and all those challenging times are distant memories.

Chapter 6
The Six Areas of Life

"Whatever you vividly imagine,
ardently desire, sincerely believe,
and enthusiastically act upon must
inevitably come to pass."
—Paul J. Meyer

Paul J. Meyer, founder of Success Motivation Institute, Inc., was the author of a number of great courses on success, goal setting and communication.

In his course on goal setting, he talked about the importance of having balance in your life. It's not easy to do. But I think having a balanced life is certainly a worthy ideal for which to strive.

Meyer broke things down into six areas, and I think these six areas provide a great place to start in creating your Vivid Vision for your Best Life. Feel free to alter them as you wish, but I think, generally, you can place all the parts of your life in these six areas.

These six areas of life are:

1. Financial and Career
2. Physical and Health
3. Family and Home

33

4. Mental and Educational
5. Social and Cultural
6. Spiritual and Ethical

Financial and Career

This is the area where most people have the most goals as opposed to the other five. Consequently, this is where most people get out of balance with the rest of their life.

As you might suspect, Financial and Career is anything to do with money, job, earnings, business, advancements, debt, net worth, retirement and investments.

How much money do you want to make? How much do you want to have in your investment accounts when you retire? When do you want to retire? When will you be out of unsecured debt? When will *all* debt be eliminated—both secured and unsecured?

Do you want to own a business? What kind? Where? How big? Whom will it serve? What will it look like?

How will you utilize your best skills, talents, knowledge and experience to serve others?

What does a day in your life look like with your finances and your career as you envision them?

And don't forget your attitudes and beliefs about money and career.

Physical and Health

This area is all about your physical and mental fitness. How do you imagine your health throughout your life? How active do you want to be?

What frailties or health challenges do you wish to overcome?

Think about all of it. Your teeth, your skin, your eyes, your hair, your weight, your blood pressure, energy level, stamina and strength.

How about your mental health? And your EQ—your Emotional Intelligence?

What's your vision for your ideal, overall health?

Family and Home

In my mind, family means the family you have as well as the family you plan to have. Your close family and your extended family.

How do you want your familial relationships to be? What is your relationship like with your partner?

The person you choose as your mate is one of the biggest decisions you will ever make. And if you've already made it, then making it the best you can make it is paramount.

Describe your relationship with your kids and their relationship with each other. This is your life, your canvas. And you get to paint it with all the rich colors available in the Universe.

Where do you want to live? What part of the country? What climate? What community?

Describe your ideal home in detail, yet with room to accommodate even more than you can now imagine.

What's your ideal day with your family in your home? Feel the pride, the joy and the satisfaction of your best home environment.

Michael E. Angier

What kind of car(s) do you drive? How do you feel when you drive your vehicles?

Mental and Educational

I believe your best chance for staying sharp and current is to commit to lifelong learning.

What are your formal education certificate and degrees? What will you be doing on an ongoing basis to stay abreast of your industry and interests?

How will you keep your mind sharp? What will you do to remain stimulated?

What do you want to learn to do? What skills and talents do you wish to master?

Social and Cultural

What are your friendships like? Who are the people you spend time with? How do they support, inspire and uplift you—and you them?

What do you do socially? What do you do for fun? How often?

Describe your vacations. How do they nurture, refresh and rejuvenate you?

What are your philanthropic endeavors? How do you give—and to whom?

Spiritual and Ethical

What do you do to nourish your faith? How does it feed you?

What are your ethics? How do you commune with nature?

This is your life, your beliefs, your choices.

All these areas are important. And I'm betting there are some of them that you haven't thought about as much. But together, they all make for a rich and rewarding life—your best life—balanced.

Author's Note: Yes, it's true, I did not use the exact format above for my own personal vision statement that I shared in the previous chapter.

But I would if I was starting it today. And since I'm now in a different phase of my life (the Golden Years), I may very well start over with the six areas as a template.

Action Step

Put these six areas of your life into a computer document and start to fill in each area by answering some of the questions I asked. Don't worry about getting it perfect. Just start writing and edit and add more later.

Michael E. Angier

Chapter 7
Writing Your Vision

"No matter what your past has
been, you have a spotless future."
—Hugh B. Brown

Your vision statement should be your best possible outcome. Remember that the purpose of your vision statement is to inspire, motivate and stimulate creativity. It's not a goal or an objective; it's a vision.

It should be big. And scare you—at least a little.

Make it Emotional

People are emotional beings. Emotion is literally *energy in motion*. By using emotional words, we charge our vision with passion.

The more sensory details you use, the more powerful your statement will be. Use color, sound, shapes and scenes. These details will help you construct a more complete and powerful mental image of your intended outcome.

Make it Present Tense

Your vision statement is most powerful if it is written in the present tense. Describe it as if it were already accomplished.

That's important because that's what a Vivid Vision should do—get you to feel strong emotions.

As you saw from my own personal Vision Statement, I used the narrative approach. I like the narrative because it feels like more of a story, and it's easier for me to use descriptive language that evokes feelings and emotions.

That's the whole point of affirmations and visualization. They are simply tools to get you to tap into your powerful emotions of desire, love, determination and more.

As The Pharaoh said in *The Ten Commandments*, "So let it be written, so let it be done."

The List Approach

Having a Vivid Vision that is a list of all you want in your life is OK, too—especially to start with.

Most people don't like to write all that much. So if making a list (especially if it includes pictures) seems less daunting, go that route.

The important thing is to get started. You don't need to get it all done in one sitting—or even five or six. This is a living, breathing document. And as you ponder the possibilities, you find more to add, refine and edit.

Vision Board

This concept is discussed in Chapter 10.

Fill In All the Areas

Using the six areas from the previous chapter, begin to paint a picture of your balanced life. Describe the highest and best experiences and accomplishments for each area.

A Look Back

It might be helpful to imagine yourself as an 80-year-old person looking back on your well-lived life. What will you be most proud of having accomplished? What difference will you have made?

Designer vs. Planner

Do you know the difference?

Your best life will require design *and* planning. They are closely associated, but they are not the same.

Designing is creating the vision of what you want your life to look like. As the architect of your life, you design it the way you want it to be. In doing so, you draft plans (the blueprints). The look, the materials to be used, the detail as to how things will be put together, specifications, standards, measurements, colors, etc., are all the responsibility of the architect.

But once the design is done, much more planning is still required.

Now comes the work of deciding when, where and who will do what—and in what sequence. The builder takes the blueprints and carefully lays out a plan of implementation. Obstacles and challenges need to be considered. Delays must be accounted for, with regard to materials and subcontractors. Priorities must be established and any ambiguities in the design must be worked out.

And there is plenty of time for that. Right now, I urge you to stay in the design phase. Don't worry about, or even get involved, in the planning and building stage just yet. Keep your creative design hat on and leave your hard hat hanging on the wall.

What You Don't Want

To get clear on what we want, it's sometimes helpful to think about what we *don't* want. What are the things you have experienced that you don't want to experience again? In thinking about painful, uncomfortable or distasteful things, what are the opposites to them?

For instance, if you have felt betrayed by someone, how would you describe the converse of that? Flip it around. How about, "My relationships are based in deep love and great trust. I can count on my friends and they can count on me."

See how that works?

Write Your Obituary

What would you like people to say about you and the life you lived? This tactic can wring out a few more drops of your Vivid Vision.

The story goes that Alfred Nobel awoke one morning to read his own obituary. Alfred's brother had died and the newspaper had mixed up his obituary with his brother's. And Alfred's obituary was mostly about his invention of TNT.

This was a changing day in Alfred's life. Not only had he lost his brother, but he realized that the destructive forces of TNT would be his most notable accomplishment. As a result, he committed to making a difference in a better way.

And that's why we have the Nobel Peace Prize today.

Action Step

What would your obituary say if it was written now? How would it read?

I suggest that as a clarity exercise, and in support of your Vivid Vision, you write your own obituary with all of your accomplishments of your rich and well-lived life.

Michael E. Angier

Chapter 8
Dream Big

"Dream lofty dreams, and as you dream, so shall you become. Your vision is the promise of what you shall one day be; your ideal is the prophecy of what you shall at last unveil."

—James Allen

One of your biggest challenges in this whole endeavor is to think big. In my many years as a coach and consultant, I've found most people simply don't think big enough.

Part of the reason is they think they have to see a way to accomplish their dreams before they can truly have the dream.

But that's not how it works.

The dream comes first. Reasons come second (your why); solutions and pathways come only after the first two. For some reason, the The Universe tends to hold on to the answers and only releases them to those who are sufficiently endowed with clarity and desire.

I've never met anyone who thought too big. Yes, I've encountered people who talked big and had grandiose pipe dreams, but I don't think even they believed them because they had nothing behind them—no commitment, no willingness to go after them.

This is your life and your dream. Be bold. Think large. Remember, anything is possible.

I've always loved the following quote most often attributed to Goethe: "Until one is committed, there is hesitancy, the chance to draw back. Concerning all acts of initiative (and creation), there is one elementary truth, the ignorance of which kills countless ideas and splendid plans: that the moment one definitely commits oneself, then Providence moves too. All sorts of things occur to help one that would never otherwise have occurred. A whole stream of events issues from the decision, raising in one's favor all manner of unforeseen incidents and meetings and material assistance, which no man could have dreamed would have come his way. Whatever you can do, or dream you can do, begin it. Boldness has genius, power, and magic in it. Begin it now."

Stretch Yourself

I challenge you to go outside your comfort zone and dream big. You don't grow when you stay inside your comfort zone. And stretching yourself costs nothing but a little courage.

What would be something you really want, but didn't think you could achieve? Make it part of your Vivid Vision. Because there's no penalty for not achieving it.

Chapter 9
Overcoming Vision Challenges

"The greater the obstacle, the more glory in overcoming it."
—Moliere

I think it's important to know the pitfalls, the distractions and the enemies of your Vivid Vision. In knowing them, you are better equipped to fight them off or avoid them.

Here's what I see as the most common challenges to creating and then living into your Vivid Life Vision.

Thinking Too Small

See the previous chapter for more on this issue.

Small goals are easier to believe in, but they lack motivation. A small goal says, you can have me anytime you want. But "anytime" often becomes "no time" because it's insufficiently inspiring. What's easy to do is easy *not* to do.

Make sure your vision is big enough and worthy enough of your best efforts. Otherwise you are cheating yourself—big time!

Lack of Belief

As I said in Chapter 3, You've Gotta Believe!

Michael E. Angier

In yourself, in your vision and in the power of this whole process. Creating your Vivid Vision and the strategies and tactics I've shared with you are not theoretical. They have worked for many people, and they will work for you.

Invisible Vision

One of the things that will take you off track is not keeping your Vivid Vision in front of you. Out of sight is very often out of mind.

Review it often. Keep reminders of the various aspects of your Vision. In the next chapter I will share with you how to do that.

But bear in mind that forgetting about your vision can and often does happen.

Avoid the Nay' sayers

Not everyone you encounter is going to be supportive and encouraging about your Vivid Vision for your life.

Be very careful who you share it with because even well-intentioned people can throw cold water on your dreams—oftentimes in the name of being *realistic*. If you're serious about living a big life, you can't spend time with small-thinking people. You simply can't afford it.

Chapter 10
Your Vision Board

"Vision is the art of seeing what is invisible to others."
—Jonathon Swift

One of the best ways to keep your Vision alive and at the forefront of your mind is to use a Vision Board. Some people refer to it as their Dream Board or Treasure Map.

Creating a Vision Board can be a powerful tool to help you conceptualize your goals and provides a source of motivation as you work toward your dreams.

Typically, this is a large poster board or bulletin board where you place pictures, quotes, sayings, etc., that represent the various aspects of your dreams, or in this case, your Vivid Vision.

It's not meant to replace the Vivid Vision narrative, but rather enhance it. We do, after all, think in pictures, so I'm confident you can see how this can be very helpful indeed—and fun.

Digital Vision Boards

If you'd like a digital solution to your Vision Board, you may want to try one of these solutions.

Google Keep. It's a convenient place to put notes, pictures, quotes, etc. You'll need a free Google account, but it can easily be used in any browser. www.Keep.Google.com

MS OneNote. The application I use more than any other, except email, is Microsoft OneNote. Originally developed for tablet computers, it is what I use for all my writing, note taking, brainstorming, and yes, my Vision Board. There's even a smart phone app so you can access all your important information from almost anywhere.

You can download it at no cost from https://products.office.com/en-us/onenote

Think of it like a digital 3-ring binder system with unlimited pages, unlimited page size, unlimited sections and unlimited notebooks. All indexed for quick lookups and recovery. You can thank me later.

I created a template for OneNote as a way to keep all my personal development, goals, core values, purpose, vision and mission statements, etc., all in one place.

It's called The Best Life Navigator™ and it really pulls everything together nicely. It's like a dashboard for living your best life. The Best Life Navigator will keep you much more organized, focused and directed.

The main thing to keep in mind is to have your Vision Board be a constant and uplifting reminder of the life you are choosing to live.

As a reader of this book, you can get 50% off the current price when you use the coupon code VIVIDVISION. It comes with three valuable bonuses that I'm sure you will find useful.

Full details at . . .

www.BestLifeNavigator.com

Michael E. Angier

Chapter 11
Your Core Values, Purpose and Mission

"Outstanding people have one thing in common: An absolute sense of purpose."

—Zig Ziglar

As you saw from the Path to Your Best Life graphic in Chapter One, there are two other foundational aspects to living your Best Life.

They are your Core Values, your Purpose and your Mission.

I am writing at least two more books in this series to address these very important topics.

The reason why is that your Vivid Vision will be better and more complete if you're clear on your core values, your purpose and your mission.

That said, I do have two free and one paid resource for Core Values and Mission/Purpose for you.

John Maxwell said, "Your core values are the deeply held beliefs that authentically describe your soul." And Stephen Covey said, "How different our lives are when we really know what is deeply important to us, and, keeping that picture in mind, we manage ourselves each day to be and to know what really matters most."

I believe both of these wise men.

And at www.YourCoreValues.com I share the *Top Ten Reasons to Know and Live Your Core Values.*

Also on that site, you can access a home-study course that goes in-depth into how to discover, document, articulate and live your core values. It's also available in a video course as part of the home-study course at no additional cost.

For ideas, insight and tips on how to create a motivating Mission Statement, please go to www.SuccessNet.org/mission It's a Smart Guide on how to create your Mission Statement, and I've made it available to you at no cost.

Chapter 12
In Summary

"Throughout the centuries there were men who took first steps, down new roads, armed with nothing but their own vision."

—Ayn Rand

As important as having a clear and Vivid Vision for your life is, I also believe you should enjoy the journey. You should not wait until the vision is fully realized to be happy. You should be happy as you construct this beautiful life—even when it's trying and challenging.

I love what my mentor Jim Rohn had to say about this: "Learn how to be happy with what you have, while you pursue all that you want."

"Learn how to be happy with what you have, while you pursue all that you want."

—Jim Rohn

One more word about not getting too quickly involved in the *how* you will need to realize your vision. Getting too attached to the *way* your Vision will be accomplished limits the manner in which it will all come to fruition. Focus on the results, not the path.

How Did We Do?

I began planning and writing this book with several objectives.

1. Convince you of the value and the wisdom of investing in creating a Vivid Vision for your life.

2. Try and help you to think bigger and believe in the possibilities of living up to your full and unique potential.

3. Get you to believe more in yourself, in this process and in what's possible.

4. Share resources and recommendations that will help you to create a living, breathing document that you can use as a map for living your Best Life.

5. Help you to dig deeper, think more comprehensively and eventually live in a more balanced, meaningful and significant fashion.

I hope we've been able to accomplish this together.

I wish for you to live a Vivid Life, accomplish great things and feel the happiness, fulfillment and satisfaction that comes from a life well lived.

You can do it! And you deserve it!

Have fun!

A Thank You and a Request

Thank you for reading my book! I really appreciate all of your feedback, and I love hearing what you have to say.

I need your input to make the next version of this book—and my future books—better.

Please leave a brief and helpful review on Amazon to let me know what you thought of the book. Only about one in a thousand readers leave a review. I hope you will be a one-in-a-thousand reader.

You can use this link: www.SuccessNet.org/go/amz-author

Thank you very much.

Michael E. Angier

BeYourBest@SuccessNet.org
www.SuccessNet.org

About the Author

Michael E. Angier is the founder and CIO (Chief Inspiration Officer) of SuccessNet based in the Tampa Bay area of Florida. He's a father, grandfather, husband, writer, speaker, entrepreneur, coach and student.

He's the author of the *101 Best Ways series, Best Life series, The Achievement Code,* and *The Secret to Being Fiercely Focused.*

Michael's work has been featured in numerous publications such as *USA Today, Selling Power, Personal Excellence* and *Sales & Marketing Excellence* as well as dozens of electronic publications. He's been interviewed on both TV and radio many times.

And his internationally popular articles have earned him a Paul Harris Fellowship with Rotary International.

Angier has experienced personal and professional success, but he's also suffered some bitter defeats. Although certainly preferring the former, he feels that he's learned the most from his struggles and disappointments. He feels that life's greatest lessons are learned by overcoming the obstacles in the path of a challenging and worthwhile objective.

Michael's passion is human potential. He believes fervently in the indomitable human spirit and revels in helping people and companies grow and prosper.

Over the past 40 years, Michael has devoted himself to studying what works and has been an ardent student of the principles of success. He's taught seminars and conducted workshops on goal setting, motivation and personal development in six countries.

Michael feels that there are three things essential to living a fulfilling and successful life: a purpose to live for, a self to live with and a faith to live by.

Michael is married to Dawn Angier—his partner, best friend, mentor, teacher, student and confidante. They have six adult children and five grandchildren. Michael enjoys tennis, reading, writing, publishing and helping people realize their dreams.

Mistakes Happen

We're committed to publishing inspiring, practical and professional books. However, mistakes do occur. If you should find a typographical, grammatical or factual error, we would be most grateful if you let us know. And, if you are the first to tell us about it, we'd be happy to send you a thank you gift.

Just email your find with the book name, location and type of error to BeYourBest@SuccessNet.org with "Found This!" in the subject. Thanks for your help.

Other Books by Michael Angier
www.Amazon.com/author/michaelangier

The Achievement Code
The 3C Formula for Getting What You Truly Want

The Achievement Code offers a simple, but proven, formula for getting what you truly want. With the Three C's, the author has distilled down from both ancient and modern teachers the true alchemy of success and achievement.

The Achievement Code outlines in simple, straightforward steps how to practice Clarity, Concentration and Consistency and actually get what you really want. Best-selling author, Bob Burg, writes in the Foreword, "It contains the basic principles of success upon which Michael has built his own ultra-successful life and business and upon which anyone else can do the same. In these teachings, he lays the foundation from which anyone can decide on a certain goal and by the very nature of the instruction provided, go about achieving it. In fact, if one will follow all three of the "C's" he teaches us, I cannot see how it would be possible not to succeed."

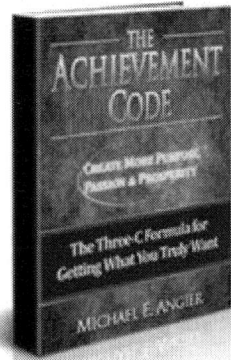

Michael E. Angier

Other Books by Michael Angier
www.Amazon.com/author/michaelangier

How to Uncover Your Compelling Core Values
Your Foundation for of a Truly Successful Life.

Your best life requires the uncovering of these values, getting clear on what they are and why they matter to you. Doing so will take you a long way toward your Empowering Purpose, your Meaningful Mission and your Vivid Vision.

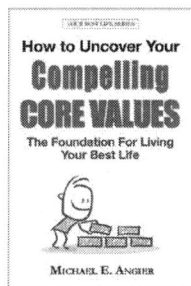

Without these Compelling Core Values, you are building on sand instead of bedrock. And that's a big reason for many failures.

This book takes you step by step through the core values process. It shows you exactly why this process is so valuable and then how to discover your top five core values, their hierarchy, and what they truly mean to you.

How to Uncover Your Compelling Core Values is based on SuccessNet's most popular online course which has helped thousands of people gain the clarity, perspective and confidence of living one's life with the integrity and conviction this process enables.

This book will help you make much better decisions. You will find yourself working on your highest priorities, getting more of the right things done with greater ease. If you want to live your best life—a more authentic, meaningful and significant life—this book is just what you need.

Other Books by Michael Angier
www.Amazon.com/author/michaelangier

Discover Your Empowering Purpose
Live Your Life with More Meaning,
Significance and Fulfillment

Mark Twain claimed, "The two most important days in your life are the day you're born and the day you find out why."

The existential question, "Why am I here?" does have an answer. You have an Empowering Purpose for your life. You only need to discover and uncover what it is.

This book helps you do that. And in doing so, you can live with more meaning, significance and fulfillment. You will have more confidence, exhibit more courage and have more commitment because you are fulfilling your purpose.

The author leads you by the hand as you determine your unique and special abilities and eventually your particular Zone of Genius.

Knowing and understanding your Empowering Purpose is a true game changer. If you're looking for more direction, inspiration, motivation, determination and devotion, read this book, go through the exercises and watch your life catch on fire.

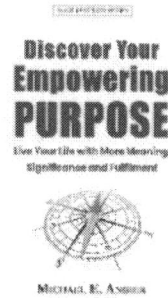

Other Books by Michael Angier

www.Amazon.com/author/michaelangier

How to Create Your Meaningful Mission

This Book is for You if You . . .

- want to maximize your time, energy and effort in a worthwhile cause—*your best life!*

- aren't satisfied with an average life— you want something bigger and better than that.

- want greater clarity for the path your life takes.

- desire to create a legacy—an exceptional life of meaning and significance—one that truly matters.

- are committed to creating a mission based upon your core values, strongly held beliefs and empowering purpose.

- desire to think bigger and believe in the possibilities of living up to your full and unique potential.

- want to believe more in yourself and in what's possible.

- want to learn about resources and recommendations that will help you create a clear and Meaningful Mission as a vehicle for living your Best Life.

- have a desire to dig deeper, think more comprehensively and live in a more balanced, meaningful and significant fashion.

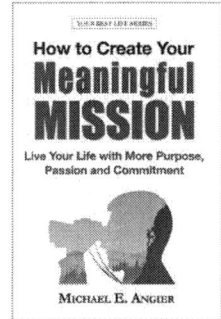

Other Books by Michael Angier
www.Amazon.com/author/michaelangier

The Secret to Being Fiercely Focused
How to Have More Energy, Less Stress and
Get More Done by Tackling Your Tolerations.

The Life-Changing Magic of Tidying Up: The Japanese Art of Decluttering and Organizing, has been off and on the New York Times Best Seller list for years—mostly on. If decluttering your home and office is life-changing, what about decluttering your *mind?*

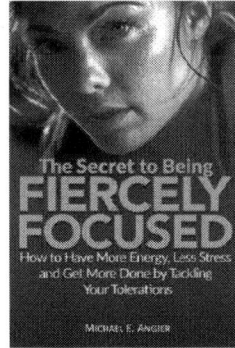

Much has been written about what you need to succeed.

But what isn't talked about much is *what you need to get rid of.*

These niggly, spirit-sucking, energy-draining, peace-killers, steal—often undetected—our joy, our happiness, our energy and our focus.

They are called Tolerations—things we tolerate, but shouldn't. And like weeds in a garden, we must recognize them for what they are and hoe them out—or they will take over our garden (life).

Other Books by Michael Angier
www.Amazon.com/author/michaelangier

101 Great Ideas to Simplify Your Life

How to Slash Stress, Ditch the Drama & Intensify Your Tranquility

Living simply is about letting go of things—ideas, activities, behaviors, items, relationships—that unnecessarily encumber the smooth flow of your life. It's about giving yourself permission to breathe freely every day.

You've heard the adage "less is more"? Simplicity is a perfect example of this principle. With a simpler life, you'll be richer. You'll have more time, more energy, more peace and more space to become the person you're meant to be.

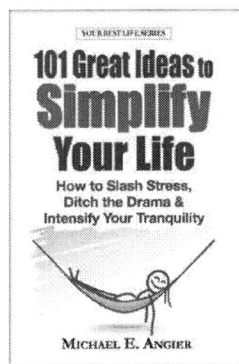

Your best life demands simplicity and clarity. And the 101 great ideas this book offers you is a cornucopia of ways to make your life dramatically better. Implement just three or four of these ideas and you will see your life start to change in a very positive way. Incorporate a dozen and your life will be transformed.

The book is filled with proven strategies, tactics and resources to help you live a simpler, more significant and more meaningful life—in a comfortable and easier way.

If you want your life to run more smoothly, have less stress and more creativity, this book needs to be in your library.

Free Resources

Personal Achievement Assessment

Download this free tool from SuccessNet. With it, you'll be able to evaluate yourself in many different areas of your life and find even more ideas in writing your life vision. Consider it your personal success inventory (PDF format).
www.SuccessNet.org/psa

How to Write a Motivating Mission Statement

A clear purpose is the foundation for your success. This Smart Guide includes examples of both personal and organizational mission statements (PDF).
www.SuccessNet.org/mission

Report: Raising the Bar

Increase your standards of excellence. Your special report may be downloaded at www.SuccessNet.org/files/raisethebar.pdf

Dedication

I dedicate this book to my father, J. Francis Angier, who at the time of this writing was 95 years old.

He always encouraged me to dream, and he helped me reach the belief that I can accomplish anything I set out to do.

He was a B-17 Bomber pilot during World War II, shot down in October of 1944, captured and held as a POW until his liberation by advancing U.S. Army forces.

After regaining most of his health, he went on to farming, flying fixed- and rotary-wing aircraft for the Vermont National Guard, married and raised five boys.

His aviation and farming career, including his combat time over Europe, is detailed in a very well-written and thoroughly engaging book titled *Ready or Not! Into the Wild Blue.*

Available on Amazon in Kindle and paperback at
www.Amazon.com/dp/B004ZGIVI8

Acknowledgements

I thank my wife, Dawn, who is my business and life partner as well as my best friend. She provided not only encouragement and feedback, but also her highly professional copy editing and technical expertise. She always makes me—and my work—look better.

In addition, I wish to thank the tens of thousands of subscribers and members of SuccessNet, who over the past 24 years, have followed me and supported our efforts in helping us all create and live our Best Lives. They are a great source of inspiration to me. And their patronage has allowed me to do work that I love for over two decades.

Made in the USA
Columbia, SC
24 January 2020